Now You Can Look

ABOUT THE AUTHOR

Julia Bird grew up in Gloucestershire and now lives in London where she works as a poetry promoter and live literature producer. She has published two poetry collections with Salt: *Hannah and the Monk* (2008) and *Twenty-four Seven Blossom* (2013).

ABOUT THE ILLUSTRATOR

Anna Vaivare is an illustrator and architect who lives in Rīga, Latvia. She has illustrated two children's books and was awarded the Jānis Baltvilks Prize for Book Art for her work in *Forage for Porridge* (Liels un mazs, 2015), a collection of poems for children by Leons Briedis. She also draws comic strips. You can find more of her work on her website: www.annavaivare.lv

While *Now You Can Look* was inspired by the lives of various artists from the 1930s and 40s, the poems are conflations of history, autobiography and fiction and do not depict actual people, living or dead.

The setting is the south of England, beginning just after the First World War. The cast list: an artist, her family, her husband, their lovers, friends and children. Uncredited extras are the writer and you, the reader.

THE EMMA PRESS

First published in Great Britain in 2017 by the Emma Press Ltd

Poems copyright © Julia Bird 2017
Illustrations copyright © Anna Vaivare 2017

All rights reserved.

The right of Julia Bird and Anna Vaivare to be identified as the author and illustrator of this work respectively has been asserted by them in accordance with the Copyright, Designs and Patents Act 1988.

ISBN 978-1-910139-84-4

A CIP catalogue record of this book is available from the British Library.

Printed and bound in Great Britain by Russell Press, Nottingham.

The Emma Press Ltd
Jewellery Quarter, Birmingham, UK
theemmapress.com

Now You Can Look

POEMS BY JULIA BIRD

ILLUSTRATIONS BY ANNA VAIVARE

THE EMMA PRESS

CONTENTS

The Artist, Aged 9, Plays a Parlour Game 2

For Her 16th Birthday, She is Taken to the Operetta 4

A Note to a Friend 6

Scenes of an Educative Nature from Her First Year at Art College . . . 8

The Assistant Escorts Her the Long Way Home Through Town . . . 10

Without Confiding in a Soul, She Goes to Get Her Hair Cut 11

She Stands in the Bedroom Doorway Wearing His Gift 12

The Artist and Her Husband Make Omelettes 15

After the Housewarming Party, She Makes a Wood Engraving . . . 16

She Makes Omelettes at 1 p.m. on a Sunday 19

The Artist in a Field in November 21

We Leaf Through Her Sketchbook 22

Scene in the Matrimonial Studio 24

They Prepare to Enter the Village Carnival Fancy Dress Competition . . . 26

She Makes Snowmen in the Garden with Her Son 27

A Bomb Damage Report 28

I Wait for My A-Level Results 30

The Artist, Aged 9, Plays a Parlour Game

Daddie is the last to finish drawing.
He puts down his pen, the mantel clock fires
a four-beat bar of chimes and that's the end of waiting.

You know this game. You draw a head and hide it in a fold
of paper, pass it to your neighbour for the body, pass it on
again for legs. On *Go!* the show of what you've made.

Daddie has drawn a daddie in three parts:
football face and a dustpan-brush moustache,
a watchchain on his waistcoat, the mirror in his boots.

Mummie's head has pigtails tied with tartan bows,
a body obscured by a rose bouquet, no legs
but petticoats and a pair of dancing shoes.

Goblin feet. Our girl bares wart-struck feet
coralled in red pencil, every blain and hangnail
detailed. She's drawn the body of a beetle

in a dozen shades from the single lead, the red
wingcase cheek-slap blush, the black spots
cochineal. And for the head —

a soldier in brass-tipped battle dress. She drew
the epaulettes, the collar and the cap
and a cross-hatched bandage where his eyes should go.

Mummie rings a bell. A pause, and then a tapping at the door.
Someone comes to clear away the tea things.
Someone brings in coal and stirs the fire.

For Her 16th Birthday, She is Taken to the Operetta at the Wintergarden

The overture to the overture
is scored Solo Gold. She lifts
her arm — her two new bangles slip,
percuss and ring. This theme,
this two-tone tuned metal song,
plays each time she moves,
plays above the foyer drone of stalls
and gods and boxes chatter, above
the programme flutter, and the ushers
guiding madam left or right.
In the gentlemen's refreshments
the icecubes snap and fracture,
and the whispering pelts
of a hundred fur coats are checked
and ticketed into the cloakroom.

In the house-lit auditorium,
the pit tunes up. A trumpeter,
Brassoing his scales, brightens
the gleam in each natural and flat
while a Brylcreemed flautist pulls
from thin air phrase after phrase
like peewit flight till the birthday girl is
breathless with his act. Through
opera glasses she lights upon
the leader of the orchestra
tightening his fiddle pegs in turn.
The scroll of his violin
is carved like the head of a lion.
He draws the bow across the strings.
Something roars. Something sings.

A Note to a Friend Regarding the Young Man with Whom She Went for a Country Walk

Dear —

Somewhat of a surprise to find that fingers such as his possessed the necessary slenderness to pick a poppy from the roadside, to pull its petals down to form a flower doll. Stamen head like a darning-snarl, nail-split stems for its legs and arms and a girdle round its waist from the single hair he flourished from his scalp. However, there it was, proffered on his palm like a penny or an aspirin or an aniseed ball.

Dear, I sped home.

Love to you all.

Scenes of an Educative Nature from Her First Year at Art College

Water

As per the assistant's instruction, she stirs her brush in a shot of blue, pulls a line across the watered page stuck to the wooden board and thus creates the sky. Colour steeps the paper, floods towards its gum-strip foot. She tilts the board and slants the sky which runs like she's made it rain.

Oil

Swept on to the canvas, her circle in charcoal has no weight till he says to think about the light and where it's falling from. Black, crude from the tube, makes a flat plane cast a shadow; titanium white is the sun, and with a dry and careful brush, she sets about blending them.

Wood

He lays the table for her — knives and gravers, chisels and a square of maple. She tricks a sketch onto the block — a sprung fern traced in reverse so her final print will turn out right — and he guides her hand as she starts to cut away the ground. The fern's already in the wood — she just clears the curls and shavings that surround it, careful that the chisel doesn't slip.

Body

A thicket of easels, unsorted, unstacked; and on every surface, jars of blown brushes, and the floor a year-long tally of paint splashes. To bottom out the classroom at the end of term takes the two of them, a mop each and buckets, and a borrowed wireless. For two hours, he scrubs, she scours — then, at the drop of her favourite dance tune she stops and stretches, pops a line of steps she makes up as she goes along, part housemaid's knee, part Charleston. She bends and kicks, he looks. He watches, and she teaches.

The Assistant Escorts Her the Long Way Home Through Town

He speaks. *I want to show you something*. Not,
it seems, the contents of this baker's shop front —
the three-deck wedding cakes and the trays of fancies
buttoned with yellow sugar roses — and not
the butcher's either. He grabs her wrist

and pulls her past a month of Sunday dinners —
chicken, pig and lamb — and on past the cheesemongers
and the oyster bar, hard against the flow of get and spend.
Here, in the window of the very last shop
at the high street's lowest end, a polar bear.

A polar bear. Ten foot of fear. Paws
black gutter hooks, gape all murder. Tongue
thick dust, eyes pressed glass, fur the colour, just,
of snow, of day-old snow, of frost on day-old
snow. Bullet-hole patched in white leather.

She stares at the taxidermist's stock — wildfowl,
fish and game, a Colorado beetle
in a box — and at the collage in plate glass:
three reflections — hers, the bear's and his.
What looks like a bite is actually a kiss.

Without Confiding in a Soul, She Goes to Get Her Hair Cut

At a minute to eleven o'clock
she is settled in the chair
in pale towels, with sweet tea
and the hairdresser saying *Ma'm'selle*
I know we spoke of this before
but are you really sure you're sure?
Their eyes meet in the same silver spot
of the salon mirror and Ma'm'selle nods.

The bun unpinned, the plaits unwound,
her dark hair sluices to the chair seat.
Its length: a tot of rag curls and pigtails
and the first time it went up; its gleam:
come from the hundred brush strokes
before bed time for a life time.
Count four with the shears and it's gone.

That evening, she carefully removes
her hat to show him from the front,
and, slowly, from the back. He blows
cut hair from her white neck, his look
a simultaneous double vow:
I don't know you and *I do.*

She Stands in the Bedroom Doorway Wearing His Gift, Saying *Don't Look Yet...*

at the yellow kimono
that's drunk up all the
colours from the room
and left it silver gelatin;
at the volume and the
line — the hem like cut
butter from an icebox
set against the billows
and the drape; at the
flowers in sewn sigils
on the borders and cuffs —
The Wreath, The Wrist
Corsage, The Unmown
April Verge; at what the
silkworm willed — giving
up its ray shagreen, its
pearl-cross mink; at the
charge — sparked from the
model like the first in

a chain of beacons being
   lit; again at the yellow
   which is topaz, rung;
   at the hooks and eyes
   of which there are none;
   at the vertical — like the
   line of lamp-light at a
   voyeur's door; the spill
   that isn't silk but skin;
   at the skin and curls;
   at the curls and silk.
   And now you can look.

The Artist and Her Husband Make Omelettes at a Quarter to Three on a Saturday Afternoon

He gets the tea trays and she sets out the tray cloths —
one with a needle-lace border, the other repeating
a thatch-roofed cottage pattern. He tells her

the story of the man who sold him quarter of a pound
of mushrooms and she sees, sliced, the black gills
and the white caps, the caps' day and the gills' night.

He dizzies six eggs with a fork in a pint-pot and she
takes down the pan which needs two hands, lights
the gas and turns its hissing lily up to full.

After the Housewarming Party, She Makes a Wood Engraving

One guest somersaults across the lawn,
another one is up the walnut tree
with a plate of buffet and the gramophone
while the hostess heads a human chain
stretching from the kitchen to the garden
serving punch in teacups in which float
sliced fruits and all the buds and sprigs
of confidences swapped and gossip spun
when a party's four hours in. A toast to the guest
twirling like a sweet-pea round a pole
as she reveals some new love's name; one
to the pair in the cabbage patch, bruising shoots
and colleagues' reputations. To those in the greenhouse,
forcing art from talk of patron and commission,
rent and exhibition: *Down the hatch.*

Cacti, succulents and vines press the panes
of the glasshouse in the background of *The Party*,
all their greens gone monochrome in the print.
That the party's done is shown by the white shoe
left on the black lawn, and the dark tree
hung with a paper lantern like a blown-out moon.
This planting scheme is jet and pearl, Dalmatian,
draughts and dice. A sunflower's fire burns silver,
snowdrops flare on Chinese lacquer stems,
and beans trace calligraphic lines. In the corner,
a marrow bed with all the vegetable stripes
turned humbug-like. With her chisel in the wood
she carves the date — 1932 —
the way a gardener will cut a word
into a marrow hide to watch it grow.

She Makes Omelettes at 1 p.m. on a Sunday

She is in the kitchen, cooking.
        He is in the attic, painting.

Rapt, he must be unaware
        of the three globed yolks in her mixing bowl

and the fourth one, ruptured on the flag floor,
        its split yellow and its blood spot.

The Artist in a Field in November

In the foothills of the unlit fire
she spots her neighbour's kitchen chair,
its seat stove in and glistening with petrol.

The wood catches, the crowd watches,
their colours wheeling round the blaze. A ring
of ruddy bodies, one of amber faces, one of charcoal coats.

A triple knot of people, warming: her, her husband
and a friend. Two dark heads and a blonde.
Look, the artist cries as a rocket rids itself of stars

and when the bang comes, both the women squeal.
That a husband whips his head towards the friend
is all it takes to show a wife

that something in her home is burning
like black timber breaking in the bonfire's core,
like Guy at its peak, flames in his hair.

We Leaf Through Her Sketchbook…

and the first few pages blister
with black ink landscapes —

                              scored and blotted cracks
                                    at the same stone wall,
                              the same bolt-struck tree

        in dead-on white daylight,
              at dusk, and
        in the dim watts of dawn.

                            Then come studies of sheepless hills
                                  done in a spectrum of snow —

        two grains of blue
      in the wash for drifts,
                dry grey

                            for the unshed fall, a nip of pink
                              as the snow salutes
                            a young midwinter sun.

Among the portraits and the likenesses,
one new face recurs: his
left profile, right profile, direct gaze.

The pages flick. He appears to grin
then frown then grin again. It's his line,

not hers, his hand that made
this drawing of a field — a flax field
bordered with a wild grass strip

parting the hawthorn hedgerow
from the crop. He's sketched

her here, touched in her tones
with soft pencil, smudged
the shading with his fingers.

The book's last pages are blank

though this green mark is dock sap

and this pressed flower, flax.

Scene in the Matrimonial Studio

Interior. Night. The contrails from their fight
still ruling off the air, but pieces of the tea-pot,

blown into cockleshells and fragments of skull,
no longer rocking where they lie. Their attitude:

squared, heads down, opposite sides of a table.
His left palm up; his inside arm, a puppy's belly,

two weeks old. She rests her fingertips
on his wrist, ostensibly to pin and steady him

although the implication is the pulse, the place
his ghost patrols the closest to the surface.

Palette. Linseed. Rags. She loads the sable brush
she'd used that night to thrust and point

and paints, in the colours of her latest work,
horizontals on his skin, starting at his watch-strap,

moving up, following not the arteries
but the veins. The paint, we understand,

is a thinned oil, loose and slick, chill
in its application, stealing blood heat

in its unction, each slow brush stroke, each stripe.
Does she catch his eye? No, she is bound to the task,

speechlessly pulling paint through the line
on his arm where the dark hairs grow and stop.

The gap below his elbow-crease is nude.
That it's space for her signature is implied.

They Prepare to Enter the Village Carnival Fancy Dress Competition

She has corn-dollied him a crown —
a weightless basket architecture, woven
with seed-heads and grasses which he wears
set square and horizontal; and he's slung
the lambskin rug over one shoulder
and his grain sack tunic is pinned
with jay and jackdaw feathers, medals
from some far-off fought campaign.

He's sprung her a pair of wings — less bird
than dragonfly — from a coat-hanger frame,
and he's glazed each pane with gold foil,
tea-dyed lace, spilt beads and yellow
silk patches. In this place, at this time,
they are Titania and Oberon. They join
the crowd of villagers and their children: Boadicea,
soldier boys and countless toddling nurses.

She Makes Snowmen in the Garden with Her Son

The snowlady, with her beads
and beach-hat, is complete.
Leaving the boy to pat more cold weight
on the snowman's chest she goes
to intercept the messenger at the gate.
He's saying what he's come to say
and the snow is melting on his cap
and there's a letter that he's trying
to give her but her hands are full
with bits of coal, a carrot and a pipe.

A Bomb Damage Report

A residential street
postal district, a
houses and maison-
lost. 29A-29D
a tooth kicked out,
from the top of a
key stuck down and
screaming note.
with their papers
cross-hatched
third-floor unhinged
of rubble. It's
the back yard now
all trees intact, each
the sun. Unmapped
road up where
standing but where

in a residential
street of boarding
ettes, one block
utterly excised like
like a tin can shot
wall, like an organ
playing one long
Burst rooms caught
showing: lilac roses,
bamboo trellis. A
door to a storey
knocked through —
open to the street,
leaf searching for
shortcut to the next
Fern Villa is still
Maple Villa is gone.

I Wait for My A-Level Results...

in a town that has a High Street
and a Cheap Street, and to hang about
them both is to live the explanation
of the market forces leading to
Black Monday, to understand
that *Romeo and Juliet* is not a tragedy
and to know ce que je veux faire
quand je grandis.

I work in the town's one gallery
and museum, where mornings I rehang
ideas on the walls — the definite
watercolours and the dithering oils —
and after lunch I dust the blackened kit
that comes from centuries of keeping shop,
ploughing fields and shearing sheep.

We don't sell postcards
of my favourite holding — the late work
by the wife of somebody you'd know.
A paper home in a glass box-frame,
each brick and roof-tile detailed
and laid on with her scalpel. Scissor-nicked
grass, torn crazy paving, brown, white
and brown lengths of Coronation bunting.

I once took a foot of till roll and cut out
eight dancing figures in a concertina.
Distracted by a customer, I tucked them
in the corner of the frame. As far
as you're aware, that's where they remain.

AUTHOR'S ACKNOWLEDGEMENTS

Thank you to Emma Wright and Rachel Piercey for all their Emma Press imagining, to Anna Vaivare for her beautiful illustrations, to *Poetry Spotlight* website which first published 'She Stands in the Bedroom Doorway', and to Mike Sims, master framer.

ABOUT THE EMMA PRESS

The Emma Press is a small, independent publisher dedicated to producing beautiful, thought-provoking books for adults and children, with a special focus on poetry. It was founded in Winnersh in 2012, by Emma Wright, and is now based in the Jewellery Quarter in Birmingham. Having been shortlisted in both 2014 and 2015, the Emma Press won the Michael Marks Award for Poetry Pamphlet Publishers in 2016.

Visit the Emma Press website: theemmapress.com